Tools

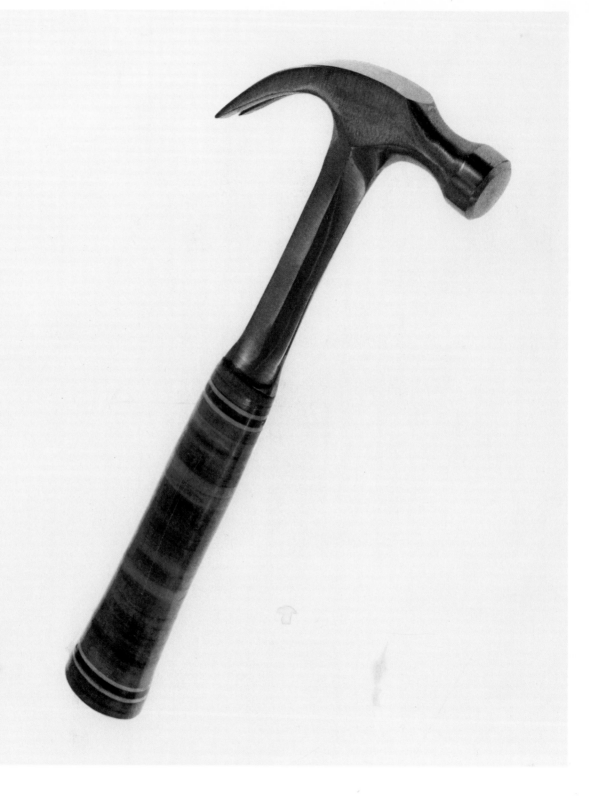

TOOLS

BY KEN ROBBINS

FOUR WINDS PRESS
New York

Copyright © 1983 by Ken Robbins.
All rights reserved. No part of this publication may be reproduced,
stored in a retrieval system, or transmitted, in any form or by any means,
electronic, mechanical, photocopying, recording, or otherwise, without prior
written permission from the Publisher. Published by Four Winds Press,
a Division of Scholastic Inc., 730 Broadway, New York, N.Y. 10003.
Manufactured in the United States of Amercia
10 9 8 7 6 5 4 3 2 1
The text of this book is set in 30 pt. Palatino.
The illustrations are black-and-white photographs,
hand-colored by the artist.
Library of Congress Cataloging in Publication Data
Robbins, Ken.
Tools.
Summary: Twenty-three full-color, labeled photographs of
tools include paintbrush, screwdriver, trowel, and pliers.
1. Tools—Juvenile literature. (1. Tools—Pictorial works) I. Title.
TJ1195.R63 1983   621.9   82-25139 ISBN 0-590-07881-X

FOR SALLY

Paintbrush

Screwdriver

Adjustable wrench

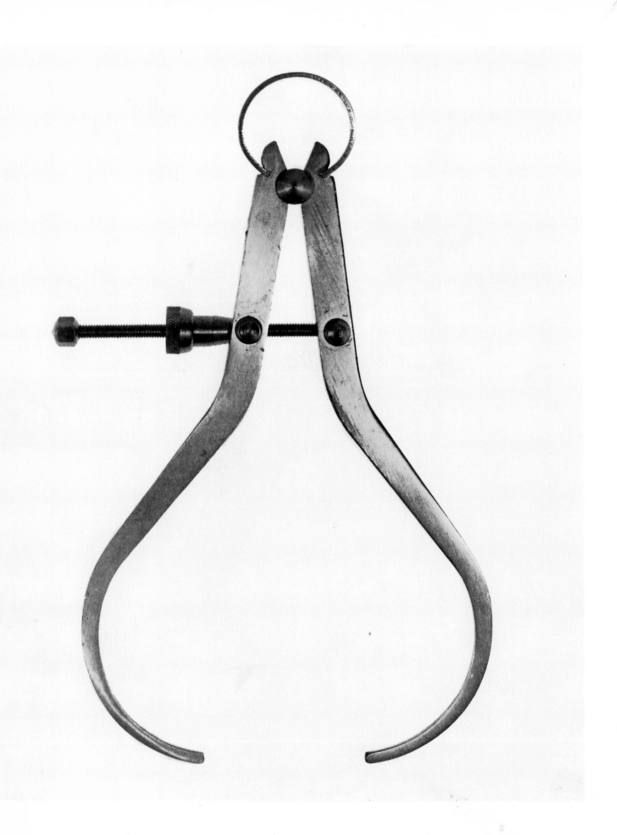

Calipers

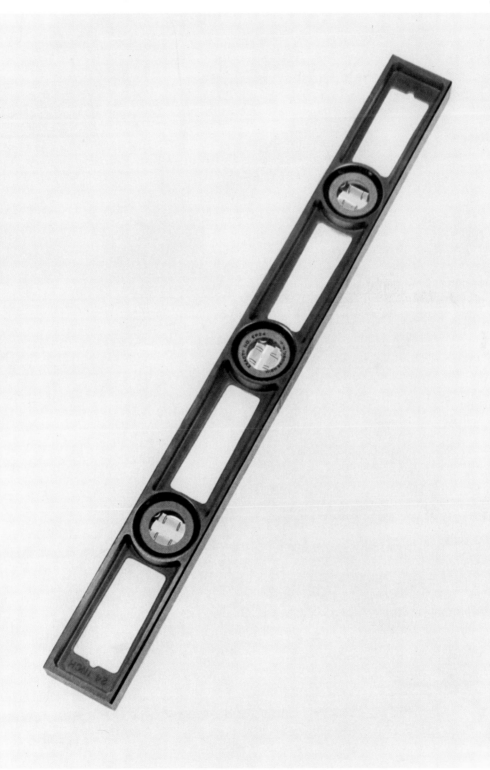

Level

Trowel

Pipe wrench

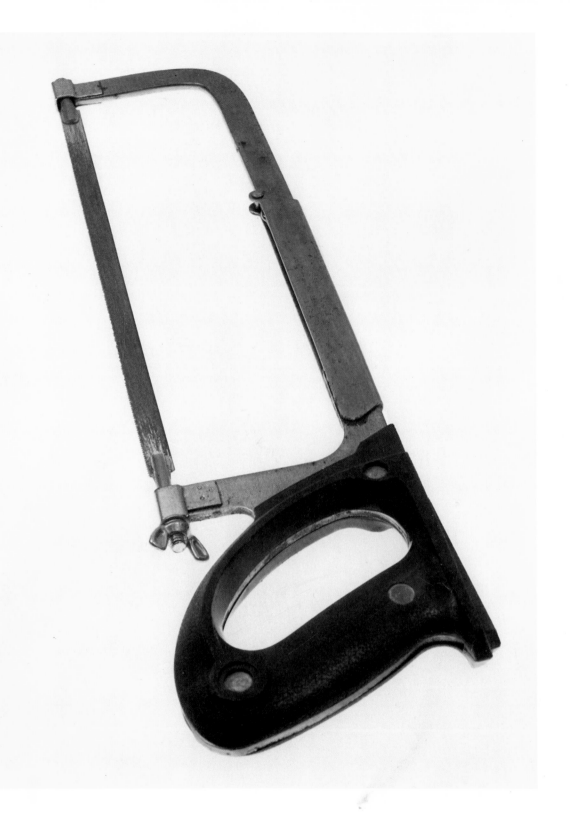

Hacksaw

Chisel

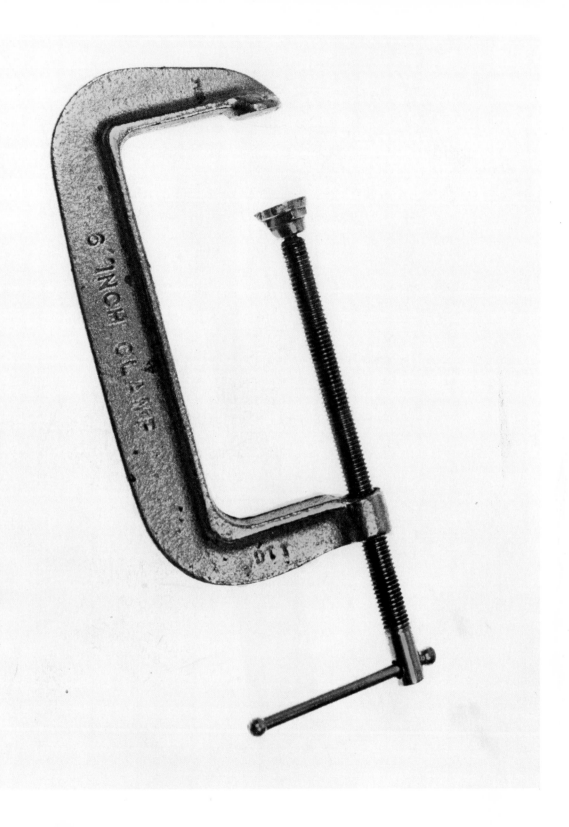

"C" clamp

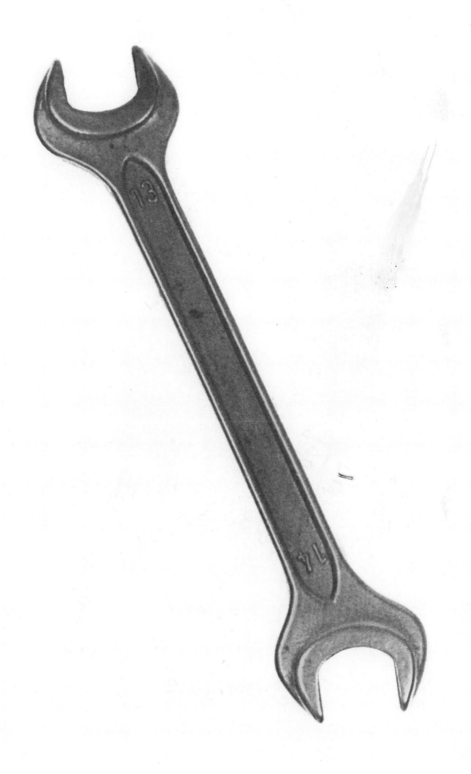

Crescent wrench

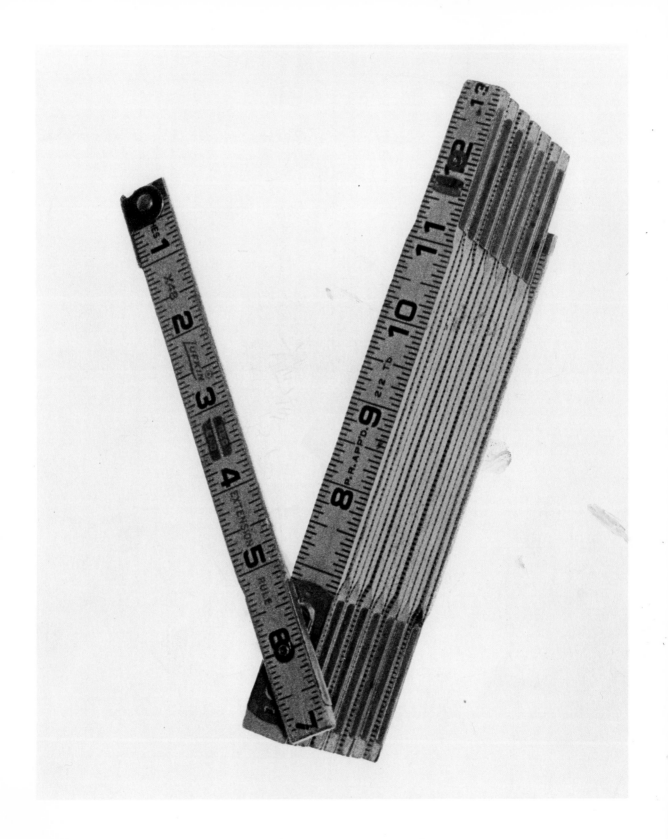

Folding rule

Metal snips

Handsaw

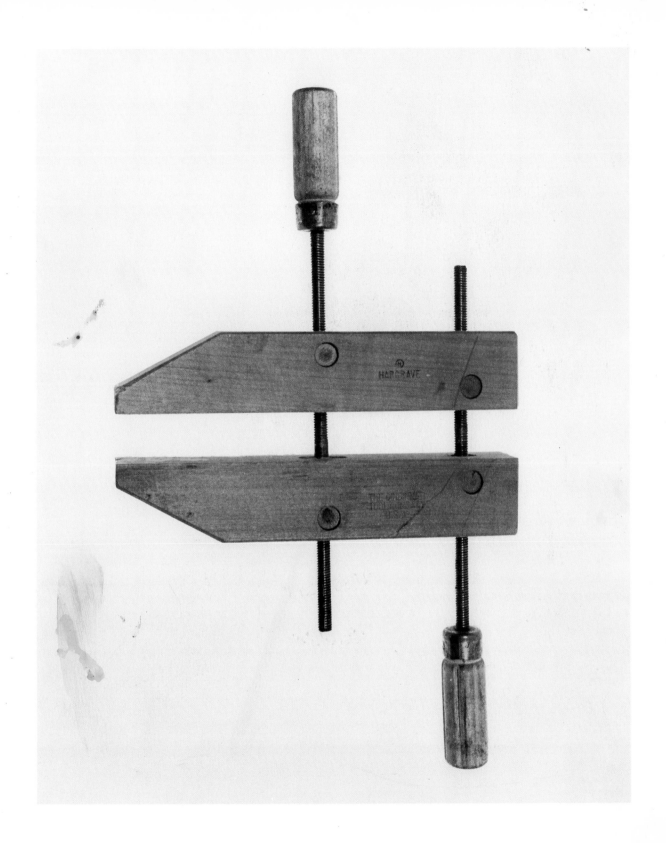

Wood clamp

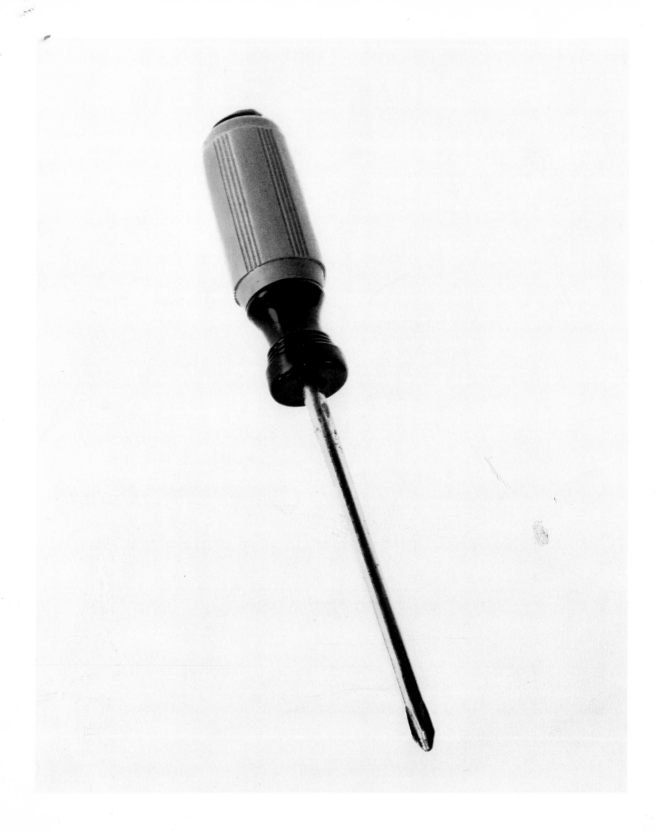

Phillips head screwdriver

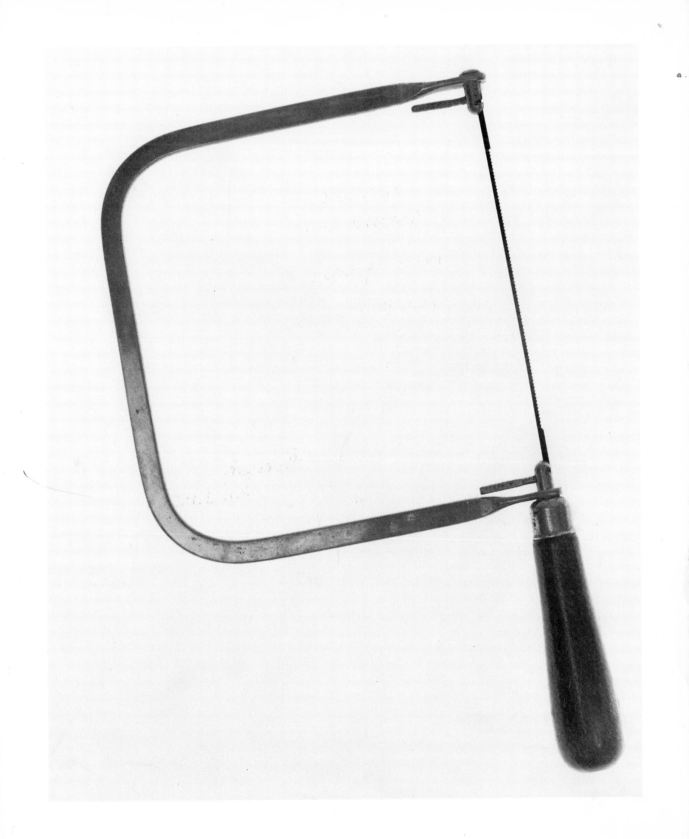

Coping saw

Plane

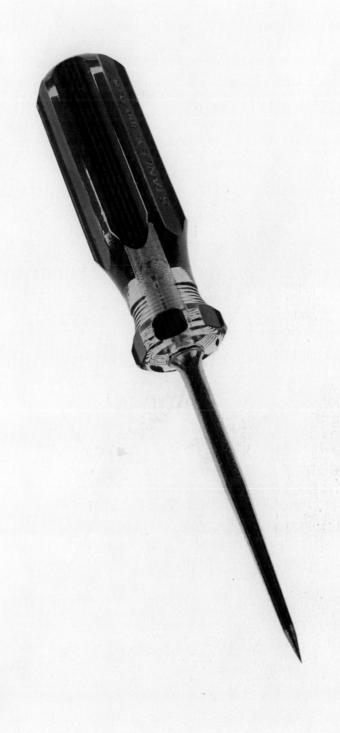

Awl

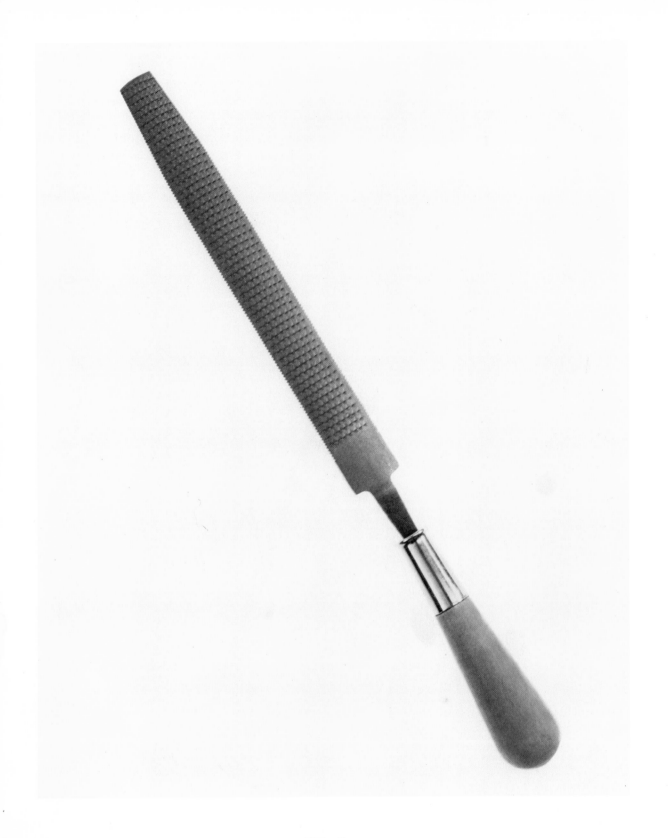

File

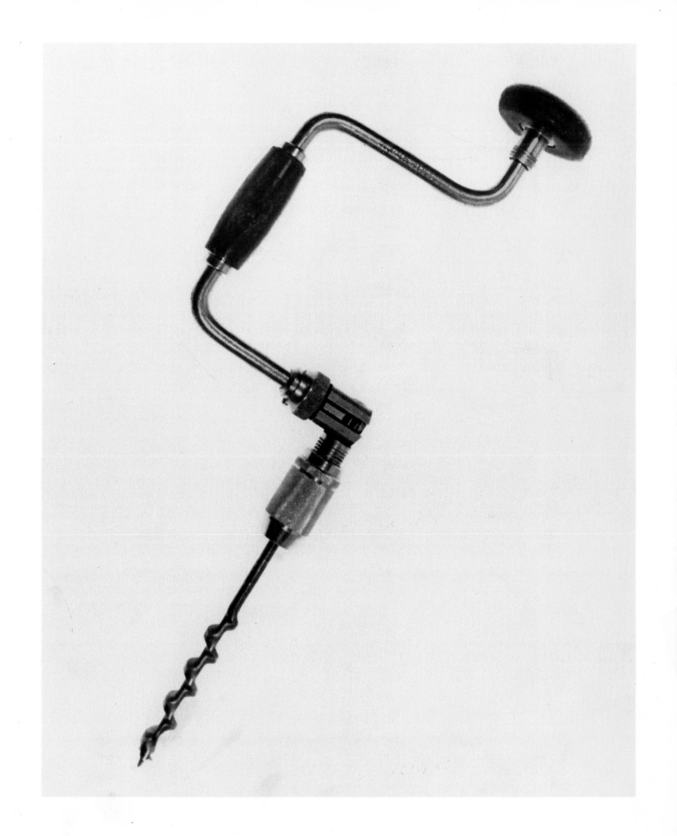

Brace and bit

Combination square

Pliers

These are tools.